OUR GARDEN BIRDS

OUR GARDEN BIRDS

A BIRD FOR EVERY WEEK OF THE YEAR

MATT SEWELL

EBURY
PRESS

9 10 8

Published in 2012 by Ebury Press, an imprint of Ebury Publishing

A Random House Group Company

Copyright © Matt Sewell 2012

Matt Sewell has asserted his right to be identified as the author of this
Work in accordance with the Copyright, Designs and Patents Act 1988

The Random House Group Limited Reg. No. 954009

Addresses for companies within the Random House Group can be
found at www.randomhouse.co.uk

A CIP catalogue record for this book is available from the British Library

The Random House Group Limited supports the Forest Stewardship Council®
(FSC®), the leading international forest-certification organisation. Our books
carrying the FSC label are printed on FSC®-certified paper. FSC is the only
forest-certification scheme supported by the leading environmental organisations,
including Greenpeace. Our paper procurement policy can be found at
www.randomhouse.co.uk/environment

To buy books by your favourite authors and register for offers visit
www.randomhouse.co.uk

Printed and bound in Italy by Printer Trento S.r.l.
Colour reproduction by Dot Gradations Ltd, UK

ISBN 9780091945008

For my goldfinches – Jess and Romy

CONTENTS

FOREWORD

I can't draw for Thorntons.* So I am always in awe of anyone who can. As a child, I would pore through my bird guides and trace them from the page. In my eagerness to worship, I would nick the outline and then devote myself to colouring them in.

So now on to someone who *can* draw. Matt's illustrations get me grinning. His obvious affection for the subject and his humour (and, heck, the *birds'* humour!), personality and character shine through in his drawings and words.

Birders (serious people with large binoculars) call this *jizz*. A term used to somehow describe the essence of the Bird. Matt's birds are the *Jizzle*.

Jimi Goodwin
July 2011

*toffee

INTRODUCTION

I've been obsessed with birds ever since I can remember, though I've never been the most active of birdwatchers, nor a twitcher chasing rare birds. But I have spent hour upon hour during my childhood immersed in bird books, pictures and postcards. Fascinated by their colours, markings and forms, I couldn't help but humanise and characterise the little treasures held within. So Buntings, Tits and Finches have always been cute, cheeky chaps; the heavy brow of Sparrowhawk left me stricken with fear, while the gorgeous pink Linnet made me swoon. As time passes and I accidentally spend joyful time with these birds in gardens, woods and through windows, it turns out that my childhood caricatures weren't too far from the truth. Every spotting tells me more and more about birds and their little ways, and I fall in love with them over and over again. I hope you feel the same way too.

THE BIRDS

Blue Tit
Cyanistes caeruleus

It's only right to start off with my favourite garden bird, the Blue Tit. What a plucky and resourceful chap: always drinking your milk, feasting at your bird table and getting cosy in your nest box. He loves us as much as we love him.

Long-tailed Tit
Aegithalos caudatus

A rather unfortunately named little
bundle of joy. But what are they?

Tiny clouds in tracksuits. I love them, and
autumn is the time of year to see plenty.
Not that most people are bothered: tell
someone excitedly that they've got Long-tailed
Tit in their garden and you'll hear nothing
but guffaws. Cretins.

House Sparrow
Passer domesticus

There's something quintessentially British about a House Sparrow (or a Spuggie, as they're known in my corner of the North). As British as chip butties and bramble picking, looking like an old RAF Squadron Leader in a flat cap and tweed. When you see them abroad they don't look right, almost like they shouldn't be there. Faded, out of place and a bit sad. Like a leathery Brit that's been in Ibiza/Thailand/Goa for far too long and lost his way. Come home!

Tree Sparrow
Passer montanus

Easily mistaken for his outgoing cousin the House Sparrow, but once you have noticed the difference you will never confuse them again. This country gentleman matches a chestnut-brown flat cap with his tweeds and prefers to congregate with his cohorts in woodland, farmland and gardens, rather than the car parks and high streets preferred by the House Sparrow. The Tree Sparrow: keeping it real, keeping it rural.

Greenfinch
Carduelis chloris

— IS IT A GOLDFINCH?

— NO.

— A YELLOWHAMMER?

— NOPE.

— IT'S NOT A BLUE TIT, IS IT?

— DON'T BE DAFT, IT'S A GREENFINCH!

— OH RIGHT, YEAH.

Greenfinches are everywhere, not that we
ever realise it. Not as green as you would
imagine, or as pretty as most finches, but
a lovely bird nonetheless, and always
welcome at the bird table.

Goldfinch
Carduelis carduelis

There's nothing more delightful than a charm
of Goldfinches, chiming from thistle to thistle
and branch to branch. And if you see one you
can rest assured that there will be a whole jolly
troop on its way. I reckon it would be all right
being a Goldfinch.

Bullfinch
Pyrrhula pyrrhula

Sandwiched between a Goldfinch and a Siskin,
it's not hard to picture the Bullfinch as the
behemoth of the bird feeder, all neck and beak,
ready to kick in the head of any poor soul
looking for a few seeds.

But come wintertime, when he's more likely
to be visiting bird feeding stations, you will
see that the depictions in bird books just don't
hold up. His playful yet shy buoyancy, petite
frame and lovely low-pitched beep of
a song far removes him from that image of the
elephantine brawny-finch. The colour-combo
of his vivid pinky red breast and the black-as-
coal balaclava is graphic perfection. He really
is as enchanting a bird as anyone would hope
to meet and I, for one, am wishing for a longer
winter this year. I'm besotted.

Siskin
Carduelis spinus

If you have a small crop of pine trees nearby
you may already be acquainted with the
delightful Siskin. A sound northerner who has
a habit of leaving the woods to pop in on local
bird feeders and relieve them of nuts and seeds.
Think of a Greenfinch's small Scottish cousin
heading out on a winter break.

Great Tit
Parus major

Probably our most unfortunately named
garden bird, not that he cares. The most
handsome and proudest of the tits, mainly to
be found bossing the other birds around and
letting everyone know the news with one of his
many songs.

When you're out and about, you might hear
a birdsong that is cutting through the traffic
din – but you can't for the life of you work out
who it is singing so loudly and brightly. Nine
times out of ten, that unidentifiable bird will
be a Great Tit.

Chaffinch
Fringilla coelebs

Very pretty but common as muck. The
scrounger of crisp crumbs, they loiter round car
parks at beauty spots, and even before you've
got your boots off they're on your car and after
your lunch. Not that they will take any bits
from your hand, they're not that brave.

Brambling
Fringilla montifringilla

This forest and woodland dweller can often be spotted in a garden, lured in by the promise of sunflower hearts. A beautifully attired bird who could easily be mistaken for a Chaffinch wearing Arran knitwear and a Zorro mask. The latter is favoured by the males around breeding time to attract the lady Bramblings. I bet they smell like roast chestnuts.

Yellowhammer
Emberiza citrinella

A gorgeous summer bird, cute as a button
made of butter but as nervous as a fireguard
made of chocolate. Many can be spotted
whilst on our countryside strolls, not that
the Yellowhammer likes our company – he
just thinks we are following him. Mainly to
be found in allotments, fields and hedgerows,
frantically chirping his 'chi chi chi' song, which
I think roughly translates as 'help! help! help!'.

This little bunting needs to learn how to relax.

Woodpigeon
Columba palumbus

Like a half-cut grandad, proud as punch at his granddaughter's wedding; in a brand-new suit, having the time of his life, stuffed to the gunnels with booze and cake, and getting ready to take to the dancefloor. But watch out, because if you have ever been near a Woodpigeon taking off or landing in a tree you will know it's not a pretty sight. And if you don't see it coming you could be forgiven for thinking that a tree is about to topple down onto you... Run for your lives!

Collared Dove
Streptopelia decaocto

A very lovely, peaceful and polite bird that
is a regular fixture in many of our gardens
and parks. He's a true world conqueror who
has naturally spread his wings and colonised
just about everywhere between here and
his humble beginnings in India – strangely
enough, given that he is not a migratory bird
and is a pacifist. So it's true what they say:
good manners can get you very far – global
domination in fact.

Sparrowhawk
Accipiter nisus

The Sparrowhawk is built for one purpose
only: the capture and destruction of small
birds; stealth and power wrapped up in one
fearsome Panzer Tank body with wings.
The male wears battleship grey and his cruel
ladyfriend camo brown, with long raptor legs
and heavy frowning eyebrows. They come
out of nowhere to take their prey in a blitz of
terror, leaving a puff of feathers and distant
cries for help. The aftermath of shock lingers
long among the surrounding birds and spotters
alike, who had just one second ago been
watching a lovely little Blue Tit tucking into
a new lardy ball! Not any more.

Terrible fables surround these phantoms; some
say they eat their prey whilst it is still alive and
others tell that they only eat the poor little
birds' brains. A true TerrorHawk!

Pied Wagtail
Motacilla alba

With a hop, skip and a jump the Pied Wagtail
is instantly recognisable. Always on the move,
always on the go, bouncing here and there to
catch the tiniest of flies, with utter joy and
ease. He takes his job very seriously and you
can see he thinks it's the best job in the world.

You can be sure he sleeps with his foot tapping,
dreaming of mayflies and midges.

Redwing
Turdus iliacus

Redwing looks like a thrush that mistook
a can of red spray-paint for his deodorant
and headed out for the day.

A band of Redwings can often be spotted in
the autumn in your garden, attempting daring
daylight raids on holly bushes. Maybe it's the
holly berries that give him the healthy glow.

Hoopoe
Upupa epops

A very rare bird and only an occasional visitor
to the British Isles, but such an amazing
and beautiful bird that he finds his way into
many British bird books. From the first
millisecond glimpse of a Hoopoe you know
he doesn't belong here. He should be back in
the Mediterranean, sunning himself on those
beach-towel wings and getting his crown
waxed – not slumming here with the everyday
pidgins and passerines of the bog-standard
British summertime.

House Martin
Delichon urbica

Though they almost seem cut from the same
cloth as their high-speed cousins, they're not
quite as dashing as a Swallow or as unearthly
powerful as a Swift. But with a name like
'Martin' how could this be anything but
a lovely, friendly bird? They live practically in
our own homes, nesting up in the eaves and
gable ends of houses in muddy cup nests.
But they're never, ever a nuisance, spending
their summery days frolicking mid-flight while
snatching insects on the wing, making flying
look like the joy we know it would be.
They are also very handy for predicting the
weather: if they are flying high then it's going
to be a lovely, sunny day; if they're flying low,
take a brolly.

Swallow
Hirundo rustica

It's true what they say, one Swallow does
not make a summer, but a whole telephone
wire full of these fellows manically chirping
their conversational song does. Almost as
soon as he's here and we've just got used
to his delightful presence skipping over the
hedgerows and skimming over the river,
then he's gone, leaving the place a little bit
duller. Like an old friend who returns for the
summer, fills the whole room with love and
laughter, then before you know it disappears
into the sun on another merry adventure. You
don't want to clip his wings and make him
stay against his wishes – that would be totally
unjust and a terrible thing – but just a tiny,
little bit more time would be lovely... Then
again there is always next summer to look
forward to... or, please, just take me with you.

Swift
Apus apus

A bird made to fly. Like a bow that took flight with the arrow, he is always to be seen screaming through the summer skies. Often mistaken for a Swallow or Martin, the Swift isn't even in the same family – in fact, he's more closely related to Hummingbirds and another curiosity, the Nightjar.

The Swift is a strange one as he is so unlike other birds. Many odd claims are made about him: he spends more time in the air than any other bird, he feeds and drinks exclusively in the air, he collects his nesting materials whilst in flight, and he bathes, mates and sleeps whilst on the wing. A definite myth is that the Swift doesn't have feet; that one is not true – he just has short legs.

Waxwing
Bombycilla garrulus

A winter visitor, seeking warmth in our cold climes from the even colder snowscapes of Scandinavia. Waxwings blow my mind. I've always been skeptical whether these birds exist or not. They're like a computer-generated samurai finch designed by a norse god. Those little red waxy droplets are amazingly improbable; their faded colourway, menacing headwear and dark warpaint are, surely, too bewilderingly accomplished to be the product of evolution.

But a spot of a Waxwing will always be a good one as they stick together and strip rowan bushes over the course of a frenzied few minutes. Try to get close as they're not that bothered about you. Not *too* close, mind: nobody knows *what* they are capable of.

Dunnock
Prunella modularis

Poor old Dunnock. You never hear anybody
saying, 'Oh, I saw a lovely Dunnock this
morning.' Looking not unlike a drab Sparrow
on a bad day, this fellow goes largely unnoticed
in the garden. But if you disturb one you will
certainly know about it, as this little blunderbuss
packs almost as much of a punch in his song as
the Wren. They might not be much to look at
but they certainly are mighty little gasbags.

Firecrest and Goldcrest
Regulus ignicapillus and *Regulus regulus*

The smallest birds in Britain, they're so tiny
this *v* is the actual size of their beaks and the
dot from this *i* is the same size as one of their
precious little peepers. Or *ivi* for a life-size
version. They weigh roughly the same as a
teaspoonful of sugar, a mouthful of air, or
a funny idea. Even though they are practically
identical, the Firecrest wears his bright flat cap
in a youthful, stylish backwards fashion, whilst
the Goldcrest keeps it classic and wears his
forwards at all times, as all gentlemen should.

Wren
Troglodytes troglodytes

Like Blackbirds, gnomes and roses, no British garden is complete without a Wren. A tiny, busy, hardy bird that won't mind telling anybody of any shape or size to sling their hook. With a voice that can cut through glass, Wrens rule their corner of the garden. But despite all their boisterousness and front, there is no cuter sight than a family of young wrens moving through the undergrowth, like a moth gently being followed by pieces of soot.

There is a louder Wren on our fair Isles though. Take a boat to the archipelagos of the Outer Hebrides and here, thriving in the bitter North Atlantic wilderness, you will find the St Kilda Wren. This larger Scottish cousin has a noticeably louder voice as he needs to be heard over the maelstrom of the ocean. The island was evacuated in the 1930s and the St Kilda Wren's numbers have been on the rise ever since. Good news.

Crow
Corvus corone

Crows have been followed by malice, fear and
omens since the beginning of time. Maybe
it's their penchant for feeding upon corpses
that earned them this bad rep, outcasts going
about their nest-raiding and fledgling-hunting
alone. They have a tough black exterior and
an even darker menace lingering on the inside.
They're jet black, darkest-night black, with a
black beak so mighty it gave us the name of the
burglar's favourite tool: the crowbar.

Rook
Corvus frugilegus

It's almost as if they shouldn't belong to the
Crow family; sociable and generally vegetarian,
Rooks are just out for a laugh, really. With a
clownish, daft face and a shaggy, dishevelled
appearance, these croakers aren't out to cause
mischief like their cousins. In fact, when not
in their rookery they spend most of their
time in fields, not being scared by scarecrows
(maybe if all the farmers got together and
changed the name to 'scarerooks', that would
work better). But farmers should just leave
them alone as they eat as many pests and crop-
eating bugs as they do seeds. Good old Rooks.

Jay
Garrulus glandarius

Maybe it's the mischievous glint in his eyes,
maybe it's his floppy flight from tree to tree,
or maybe it's that flashy streak of blue on his
wings. Whatever it is, there is a look to
a Jay that says he is up to no good – nothing
too bad, but enough to earn him a bit of a
reputation as a scallywag and a roustabout.
Nevertheless, it is always a joy to spot a Jay,
even more so in towns and cities where his
numbers are on the rise.

Jackdaw
Corvus monedula

The least creepy of the crows, often seen
swaggering about like he's carrying a couple
of radiators. His brothers the Crow and Raven
definitely have the whole horror thing sewn
up, but there is still something a bit spooky
about a Jackdaw.

He is one of the only birds to have white
irises and, like humans, he uses eye contact to
communicate. That's why, if you're walking
along and a Jackdaw looks you directly in the
eye – almost like he's reading your mind –
you'll feel slightly unsettled before he flies off.
The Jackdaw: never afraid to hold a man's gaze.

Green Woodpecker
Picus viridis

Of our three woodpeckers on the British Isles, the green is the most instantly recognizable. His plumage makes him hard to detect whilst up a tree, but once this guy leaves the camouflage of leaves he's like a neon powerball bouncing through the thicket.

There is nothing surreptitious about the Green Woodpecker; he flies like a madman up and down, up and down, and when he's not banging away at a tree with that beak, he's calling loudly with his piercing 'yaffle' laugh. ('Yaffle' is an old English name for the bird, as in Professor Yaffle, Bagpuss's friend.)

So what makes him such an extrovert? Maybe it's the extra-long tongue he hides in his beak – it can apparently stretch his body length to reach bores, beetles and weevils. Personally I think he'd be more at home with a can of lager and a kebab!

Great Spotted Woodpecker
Dendrocopos major

At first glance you would have thought the striking graphic black, white and red colour choice of the Great Spotted and the Lesser Spotted Woodpecker wasn't too wise a decision for going unnoticed in woodland. But, gazing up through the dappled light of the forest, you can begin to understand their logic. This fellow is a lot less of a try-hard than his cousin the Green Woodpecker, keeping himself to himself, but will often be spotted in gardens swinging back and forth on bird feeders built for little finches.

Robin
Erithacus rubecula

The quintessential winter bird. He's actually
with us all year round, as most gardeners will
know, diving in around your wellies for grubs
and worms even before the spade has left
the earth. The grandmother's favourite, but
everybody loves him. Charming and cocky,
with his shocking-red vest and a song
like Sinatra's.

Redstart
Phoenicurus phoenicurus

Definitely one of the most dashingly
handsome of the garden visitors, he can easily
give his cousin the Robin a run for his money.
They are very much cut from the same cloth,
but the Redstart ain't half as bossy or nosey
as the Robin. He just darts about with his
lady-friend, flicking his beautiful orange tail.
And what a lady she is, my word, by far the
prettiest of all the female little birds. Any
amount of time spent gazing upon this fair
maiden is worth its weight in gold.

Barn Owl
Tyto alba

Renowned since antiquity for its links with
magic and mystery but also a portent of
doom and tragedy, the Barn Owl is a night
animal that strikes cold terror into the heart
of whoever hears its screech. Symbolism
and witchcraft have given owls such bad
press, especially the Barn Owl. In truth he is
completely magical and otherworldly in his
gold, silver and white, shimmering silently
through the dark night like a royal ghost. He's
also the sweetest of owls, whose face can be
drawn as a heart with two huge round eyes.
However, I must warn you about Barn Owl
chicks: do try your best not to look at them,
they are rather hideous.

Tawny Owl
Strix aluco

Perhaps the wisest of all owls, or the wisest-looking anyway, especially when spotted during the day half asleep, like an old professor caught napping in his study. The Tawny Owl seems very huggable; it's hard to resist going in for a cuddle until you see those talons and fearsome beak hidden behind all the fluff.

Tawnys are responsible for the classic 'to-wit to-woo', but I'm informed it's not actually one bird making that song: the male makes the 'to-wit' and a lady calls back 'to-woo'. It's just nice to know there are so many around.

Nuthatch
Sitta europaea

You would be forgiven for thinking somebody
has played a practical joke and stuck a door-
stop on the bird feeder when you first clap eyes
on the blue wedge that is a Nuthatch. He looks
much bigger than most tits, finches and tree-
hopping birds but he's not: he's just all beak.
When he isn't using it to protect his claim
on the bird feeder, he's using it to crack nuts
whilst running up and down trees. He makes
that familiar woodpecker knocking sound too,
so have a closer look next time you hear 'tap
tap tap' – it might just be a Nuthatch getting
stuck into some grubs.

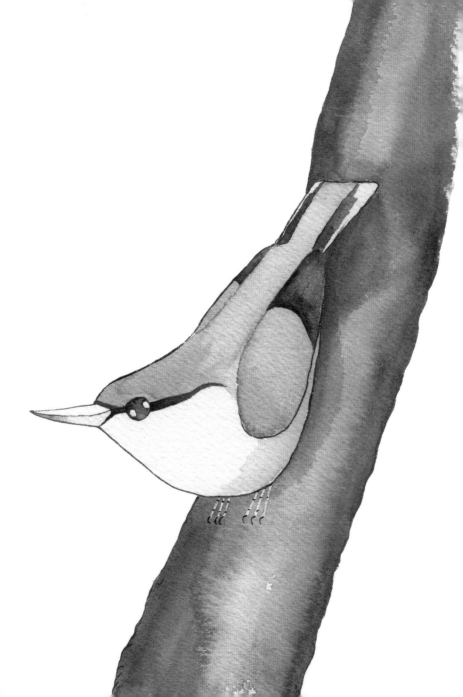

Treecreeper
Certhia familiaris

Distantly related to the Nuthatch, the
Treecreeper possesses the same dexterity on
the tree trunks and branches of the garden
as his bigger, far-removed cousin. But he's
altogether more tiny and diminutive, like
a mouse crossed with a hummingbird,
scurrying all over the tree using his long beak
to pick out and feast upon lovely delicacies as
spiders, moths and earwigs. You can often spot
a Treecreeper in the winter months hanging
out with the big boys for protection – his pals
the Great and Blue Tits.

Starling
Sturnus vulgaris

A very curious bird that not many people recognize up close. Much cleverer than they look, they are closely related to world-famous mimic the Mynah Bird and other mockingbirds. Most of us know Starlings for flying in flocks around the cities, painting rooftops and statues white – rather than for their amazing, oil-slick-of-iridescence 'coat' and breathtaking air displays. Just before dusk in certain areas thousands of Starlings meet up to perform a morphing sky dance. As a single dazzling, undulating mass they say you a big 'thank you' to the sun before they roost for the night.

Song Thrush
Turdus philomelos

How many songs does a Song Thrush know?
Only one but he sings it so well. Each bird
adds to and riffs on the same song year by year,
with the epic melody becoming more brilliant
and sparkling with every passing summer.
A frequent visitor to the garden and a welcome
one too, he helpfully pounces on snails of all
shapes and sizes, and joyfully smashes them to
pieces right by your feet.

Blackcap
Sylvia atricapilla

As warblers go, there's never that much to call
upon to distinguish one from the other. I have a
terrible time spotting the difference between
a Wood and a Willow Warbler, for example. But
the Blackcap certainly knows how to stand out
from the crowd, as he pulls on his jet-black hat
and heads out for the day. Even with a power-
dressing move like that, the Blackcap is as shy,
retiring and hidden as any other Warbler –
every bit as handsome and elegant too.

Chiffchaff
Phylloscopus collybita

Often to be found at the top of a tree singing
his little heart out, the height makes him
even harder to distinguish from his warbler
brothers. But listen to his song and you will
see why his moniker is apt: not just Another
Warbler, he calls out loud and clear, 'CHEEF
CHEAF, CHEEF CHEAF, CHEEF CHEAF'.

Blackbird
Turdus merula

A healthy addition to any garden and a resident in most. Just by listening to the Blackbird's call, you can tell what's going on out there: whatever is happening he likes to sing about it. Danger, happiness and general comings and goings are all reported on, and of course he welcomes the sun each and every morning. The Blackbird sings with compassion, clarity and heart.

Like his song, the Blackbird is a bold character and is at the forefront of all goings-on in the garden. He likes to think he's the boss, ruling the roost and protecting his patch with glee.

Coal Tit
Periparus ater

Like a faded Blue Tit who's pulled his head
out of a bottle of coal dust rather than milk,
it's easy to distinguish him from his brighter
Titmouse cousins. Like Goldfinches, the Coal
Tit prefers to spend his time in great flocks,
flitting between woodland, gardens
and orchards, making for a gorgeous sight
to behold – lucky us.

Nightingale
Luscinia megarhynchos

Not much to look at, but as with all true
beauty it is what's inside that counts. What
is inside this lady is a divine call, a gift of a
long, beautiful song. She's rather Robin-like in
appearance and gesture, but not one fraction
as common. Even with such small numbers
and rarity, the Nightingale's angelic aria has
inspired poets, artists and lovers since the
beginning of time.

Linnet
Carduelis cannabina

Cute as your first crush. In pink and beige
the Linnet is a slight and endearing finch,
mainly to be found in dense spiky bushes and
hedgerows. Come the summer months
a gorgeous sight is a handful of Linnets
skipping through a wild meadow and gossiping
like a group of old girlfriends who haven't seen
each other in years and have sooo much to talk
about. Twitter twitter twitter.

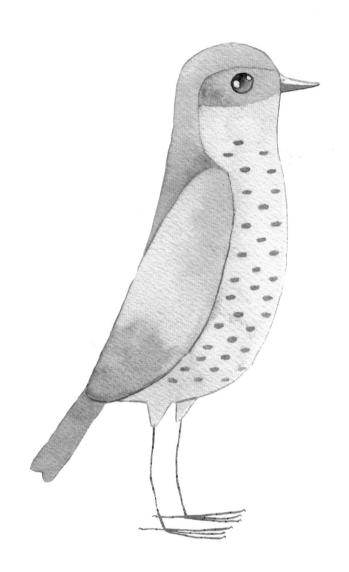

Mistle Thrush
Turdus viscivorus

The ghostly apparition that haunts your
garden and disappears back into the woods is
a Mistle Thrush. Legend has it that he is the
ghost of a storm cock who tried to warn people
of a deadly tempest on the way – he was torn
from his tree, mid-song, into the wind and
hail, with his alarm call slipping deeper into
the storm. So next time you see one, thank him
with a handful of rowanberries as he might
never do it again.

Cuckoo
Cuculus canorus

Why the suspicious look, Mrs Cuckoo? Her self-aggrandizing song is as infamous as her dubious parenting method. She forces her young upon unsuspecting parents by laying her large egg in the nest of a little Warbler or Pipit, then clears off before the unwary host parents return to their brood. They sit in hope, waiting for their enchanting progeny to join them. So loved-up are the hosts at the arrival of their first-born, they don't realise that it's a Cuckoo chick. The little hosts try to appease the ravenous brute, working night and day to feed the ever-open, greedy mouth. Shockingly, while they are away the expanding Cuckoo jettisons the true, unhatched family from the nest. The golden child is waited upon solely, and grows to four times the size of its foster parents, like a true parasite.

Aside from its brutal entrance into the world, the Cuckoo is a vital part of our landscape and national psyche, heralding the beginning of summer, and should be welcomed into our lives with open arms.

Hawfinch
Coccothraustes coccothraustes

You'd be forgiven for thinking that the
Hawfinch was some kind of autumnal bird of
prey, a killer in brown and orange. But he's
just a regular finch out to crack a few nuts.
Unfortunately that spectacular beak is set
in a permanent frown through design, as it
hinges like a natural pair of passerine secateurs
to cut through the hardest of nuts. (The fire
brigade have often called in the services of a
Hawfinch to cut through railings after some
misadventurer has got his head trapped in
them.) All in all, very pleasant – but watch
your fingers.

Kestrel
Falco tinnunculus

More commonly associated with the highways and motorways of Britain, hovering deep in concentration, as if in suspended animation. Happily they are rising in number as more of the countryside gets covered in asphalt, creating a perfect feeding ground – one good side effect, I suppose. A beautiful, feline bird of prey: the female is covered in spots like a flying leopard cub, and the male is handsome in his medieval finery, striking in grey, chestnut and black.

An occasional visitor to the garden, you're unlikely to spot one hovering above your herb patch. He most likely would have gone unnoticed, finding a quiet corner to pluck the fur or feathers from his prey in peace. More than likely the only evidence of his visit will be a light covering of downy feathers amongst your roses, as if a couple of Goldfinches have had a pillow fight.

Magpie
Pica pica

One for sorrow, two for joy. But there's never much joy when there are Magpies around, as any number spells trouble. Robbing, stealing and mugging are the name of their game. With a call that sounds like dial-up Internet and a coat of oil-slick black, this majestic crow robs nests of eggs and young, and terrorises small animals. He has a habit of liberating anything shiny and hauling it back to his lair. Like many crows he is a bird of ill omen: even today he terrifies the superstitious soul until he has been appeased with a salute or been bid a good day. 'Good morning, Mr Magpie sir, how are we today?' is the ancient enchantment you will need to keep this devilkin at bay. For now, at least.

Grey Heron
Ardea cinerea

Oh, the melancholy life of the Grey Heron,
the lonely river-man. He's a highly skilled
fisherman who is chided and chased away from
the riverbank by weekender linesmen, fearful
of losing their catch of the day to the scraggly,
sword-beaked crane. A beautiful, graceful flyer
with an immense wingspan that blocks out the
sun, he is continually mobbed by Crows and
Rooks who fear he is an Eagle or a Buzzard.
And, to top it all, he's even chased away by a
rake-shaking gardener whose pond has been
relieved of several expensive koi carp. Oh,
what a lonely life indeed. Rest assured, after
a melancholy day, every Heron flies up to his
treetop nest with the rest of his Heron brothers
and they have a good laugh about it all.

SPOTTING AND JOTTING

It's great spotting a bird you've never seen before, so here's a handy way of keeping all your jottings in check. Get spotting either by sitting comfortably at your window, or pull on some boots, grab a flask and binoculars, and go outside. Happy spotting!

☐ Blue Tit

☐ Long-tailed Tits

☐ House Sparrow

☐ Bullfinch

☐ Tree Sparrow

☐ Greenfinch

☐ Goldfinch

☐ Siskin

☐ Brambling

☐ Chaffinch

☐ Great Tit

☐ Woodpigeon

☐ Yellowhammer

☐ Collared Dove

☐ Sparrowhawk

☐ Pied Wagtail

☐ Redwing

☐ Hoopoe

☐ House Martin

☐ Swallow

☐ Swift

☐ Waxwing

☐ Dunnock

☐ Firecrest and Goldcrest

☐ Wren

☐ Crow

☐ Rook

□ Jay

□ Jackdaw

□ Robin

□ Great Spotted
Woodpecker

□ Green
Woodpecker

□ Redstart

□ Barn Owl

□ Tawny Owl

□ Treecreeper

□ Nuthatch

☐ Blackcap

☐ Linnet

☐ Nightingale

☐ Song
Thrush

☐ Starling

☐ Chiffchaff

☐ Mistle
Thrush

☐ Blackbird

☐ Coal Tits

□ Kestrel

□ Cuckoo

□ Heron

□ Hawfinch

□ Magpie

ACKNOWLEDGEMENTS

Thanks for all your support throughout
the making of this book:

Jess and Romy, The Sewells, The Roses
and The Lees.

My Aunty Val, for introducing me to
C.L. Tunnicliffe and his 'Sketchbook of Birds'.

All at Caught by the River, in particular,
Jeff Barrett for being there from page one.

And a massive thank you to all the spotters and
jotters who email me to tell me that they saw
a bird and thought of me. Sentiments don't
come much higher, please don't stop.